LOW WATER SLACK

Dave:

Nothing about
Franklin or
Vancouver (the
explorer)
here, but I hope
you enjoy them
anyway.
Thanks for
coming out.

Tim
Bowling
Edmonton
95

LOW WATER
SLACK

TIM BOWLING

NIGHTWOOD EDITIONS

Nightwood Editions
R.R.2, S.26, C.13
Gibsons, BC V0N 1V0 Canada

Cover artwork by Kim LaFave
Cover design by Roger Handling / Terra Firma
Page design & layout by David Lee Communications
Published with the assistance of the Canada Council.
Printed and bound in Canada by Hignell Printers.

Canadian Cataloguing in Publication Data

Bowling, Tim 1964–
 Low Water Slack

 Poems.
 ISBN 0-88971-161-5

 I. Fisheries—British Columbia—Poetry. I. Title.
 PS8553.O9L6 1995   C811'.54   C95-910748-7
 PR9199.3.B6L6 1995

CONTENTS

For my parents
Heck & Jean Bowling

With love and gratitude

I'd like to thank the editors of the following magazines and
anthologies where some of these poems first appeared: *Arc*,
Breathing Fire, *Capilano Review*, *Clockwatch Review* (U.S.), *Event*,
Minus Tides, *Nexus*, *Vintage 93*, *Vintage 94*, and *Westcoast
Fisherman*.
A complete list of those who have helped me write this book is
too long for inclusion here. But I hope the parties involved will
recognize themselves and accept my sincere thanks.
I'm grateful to the Explorations Program of the Canada Council
for financial assistance.

LADNER

Summer nights
Vancouver traffic rises blinking from the black
depths of the George Massey Tunnel, shifts east
and south, borne for the suburbs and the American
border; home, the familiar dream.
Rarely does a stray car break west of the
current, fumble its dice on the narrow
exit, brighten the soft felt of an evening
that has known forever the one cold gamble,
a million fortunes swimming in from the sea,
and the sound of the Fraser and the wind and
the wings of gulls, lowered human voices and
bellies rubbing swiftly over silt, all like
a long-held breath slowly exhaled. Rarely
but often enough that the red and green
fluorescent sockeye hanging in the shaggy
branches shine to advertise the prices
of the year and point the way to scale-cobbled
streets and backyard vegetable gardens draped
with shredded seine-net.

Here, beyond the exit's owl-blinking intersection,
the killing months begin. The scarlet calendar
has now been turned, and whoever you are
behind the wheel, it's far too late
to wish your senses in another season.
You have reached a town of infinite distances.
The salt that rimes your windshield
travels on the dying breath of stars,
and from the gaping mouths of the doomed
that plunge between these banks, a history
older than this world's is uttered, one
gentle tug of the moon at a time.

Past the trees of random commerce, the tidal
marsh appears, miles of bullrush stretching
over the rivermouth, the fetid moat of a
medieval castle battered to ruin by
the flashing armour of the schools. Then,
the first marina, for pleasure-craft too
sleek to know the darker truths, their
Calvary of swaying masts untouched by
blood and pain. From there, descent
across the native tongue, Chilukthan
Slough, near the spot where Thomas Ladner
raised his pioneering beams in 1868,
settling a tiny square of England on
the shifting mud of the Salish Nation.

No one's awake in the portholed houses
listing on the breeze. The streets
are cracked as the sloughed skins
of snakes. A blackberry bush offers
its small, sweet cave to the air,
and the air steps in, sighing.
It is August. The gillnet fleet
floats upon the unofficial town,
the real streets, "Prairie Drift,"
"Hole-in-the-Wall," "Port" and "Curry."
Chain-smoking gondoliers of a muddy Venice
flashing small sparks of fire, the fishermen
speak only with their calloused hands, spit,
swear into upturned collars, carriers of
the sudden dead, tour-guides to no one.
Any other night, you could find your
grandmother's name in the harbour, perhaps
your own, the bow-letters lined in moss,
the only epitaphs we'll ever know
because the ground's too soft for graves.
Orcas slide beneath our sleep like long, black
coffins, their massive tongues a satin pillow

for our final moor, and even when the deadheads
fixed in the mud begin their heavy tombstone-
turn on every tide, their wind-scarred faces
mouth no record of who or what has been;
and if they did, our present's much too swift
for laying eyelash-laurels on the past.
Yet here the world is still designed
by the ancient art of two gnarled hands,
one that slides across the silt
and one that clenches its soft blue fist
against the cattailed sky: if you should
ever pause to think about the beating
of your heart, you might hear the sturgeon
feeding on the siftings of the moon,
or feel the heron's yellow gaze
unblinking as the stars upon your bones;
these are the hands that gently sew us
into time; theirs is the long,
frail signature, continually erased
and copied again, that declares
there is no independence possible
on the river's catacombing sloughs
and the delta's watery crust of land.

But now the labradors begin to bark
in lonely chorus down the river road.
Drive faster, out of town and along
the dyke, pressed between the Fraser
and the fields of corn, netsheds wet
with the lamplight of another century
and swaybacked barns shadowing combines
crippled since the War. Here, a million
phantom horse-hooves lift from the tired
earth seeking a million silver shoes
fired on the current. They will not meet.
But slip between the missing years, go
beyond the old swing-bridge that leads

to Westham Island, climb the gravel rise
just past Swensons' farm where the rotted
pilings of the Brunswick Cannery pound
like pistons on the tide, and the breeze
blows off the Gulf of Georgia carrying
the last kiss a drowned Japanese fisherman
gave to his wife. Soon it will land on
the thousand ragged stumps and logs
washed up in the salt marsh and slowly
dry to moss. Our own breath teases
the dark hair of his crying daughter,
warms every tear on her cold cheek.
We know from what the ocean teaches
a whisper holds a dangerous thunder.

So the gillnet fishermen of Canoe Pass
stay mute on the farther shore, listening
to the salmon thrash in the nylon web.
High water runoff, and their dim mastlights
fall like shooting stars towards the sea,
blurred by the speed of the muddy plume. Now
the only human voice is what you can remember
of your own. Your car stops on the edge of
the bank, its headlights sink in the black
depths, briefly catching a glint of sockeye
as they disappear. The engine idles with
your blood; the one shuts off, the other
just begins to move, mad for home.
A harbour seal breaks the surface
of the narrow channel like a gravestone
with sad eyes, gazing at your life, imploring
courage. But the ancient hands are still and
will not form a prayer. You have reached
a town of infinite distances where the night
whispers "nothing is gained by going with
the current." This is the final welcome.
From here you're on your own.

THE TINSMITH

I

I have only seen one black man on the Fraser River
and he died in 1880, hacking up his poisoned lungs
in a Portland rooming house far from the sandheads
and marshes where he forged his minor fame. In the
fortieth hour of a two-day opening at the mouth,
when the freighters stop looming in the starlight
long enough to let the other century of our strangling
slide downstream, I see him poling a cloud of dead salmon
along the shore of the island some overworked council
forgot to strip of his name. A free mulatto from
South Carolina via San Francisco, with stops in Victoria
and the goldfields of the Cariboo, John Sullivan Deas
sang his historical moment with a tinsmith's booming
voice and cold precision, wrote unrecorded characters
in the blood of sockeye runs so large their slaughter
could accommodate a killer in a suspect skin. His cannery,
and its private drift, are only a heron's feeding flight
from where my father earned his bread in scales, and where
my oldest brother nearly drowned, madly scooping out his
plywood-skiff's rising bilge. These are the stars Deas
laboured below, this slime on my forearms dried in
similar veins upon his flesh, his tongue drew the words
"Chewassen" and "saltchuck" from the same damp air
and some long nights the pitiless moon threw handfuls
of salt in his bloodshot eyes: even the way my muscles
tense on certain tides, or when I turn my neck to feel
the swampings on a breeze, recalls a subtle flexing in
the stronger limbs of men who rowed for years against
their deaths; and why should what the body cries
not be hollered down the murky deltas of our dreams?
Suddenly, in his drifting, silt-slow gaze, I am the sky
he took his children from, the softer daybreak left behind
to light the letters of his grave.

II

Born in the antebellum south, Charleston, 1838,
free and hated. What horrors he knew were not
unique, but they belong to him and not to us.
The fact he followed his smithing skills into
the California sun, then joined the exodus of
blacks who fled the rising violence of that state
will be enough to bring him here. Or at least
to the colony of Vancouver Island, where he sought
and found to some degree "Liberty under the British
Lion." Established in Victoria, 1862, he plied his
trade, married Fanny Harris, of Hamilton, Canada West,
fathered the first of many children, bought a piece
of land, and dreamed of better things. 1866, and he
was selling goods to gold-crazed men who staggered
past the town of Yale, desperate to sluice the final
dust from the Cariboo fields. He stuck it out two
years until the rush was done, then back across the
Gulf where he dealt in stoves and hardware while
he waited for the only history he would ever have.
And the river gave it to him as it gives it to us still,
in a silver rain that blooms to roses, in a blood that
blooms to silver in our reaching hands.
For seven years, he drifted in the mouth, panning
the breathing riches of the Fraser, handcrafting
the cans for our province's first commercial pack.
From 1871 to 1878, he owned and ran a cannery on
the island that slowly took his name, fought with
Alexander Ewen, the Scottish salmon king, over
whose boats had the right to fish on different
stretches of the river, and finally lost. Then
sold out, left for the States, for the Portland
rooming house run by his wife, and died a sudden
death at 42, spewing his leaden guts until his heart
gave out, a spawner washed against the cold banks
of his skin.

III

I've only seen his eyes, and they are black
as any salmon's dying in our stern. He never
smiles, just poles his scow of fortune into
the rotted pilings of his plant, then fades
like all the other lives who built the world
we follow on this coast. If I blink, he's gone,
back to the prosaic history of his island's
single name, the only non-white canner of the
Fraser's early days. But finally, when my scaled
and weary body falls into bed and sleep, I see
him one last time, through the window of his
dying room. It's summer twilight and he can't breathe;
a warm wind flows over the sill to which his face
has turned; his supper lies uneaten on a table by
the bed. Suddenly, he hacks into convulsions that
seem to tear his vision from his flesh, and spews
a blackened phlegm into a basin. His eyes are
filled with swimming red, as though the summers
that he left intend to thrash their famous cycle
in his sight if not his hands. Outside, his seven
children school beneath a maple tree, gaping at
the upstairs gloom: even the youngest sense a
drastic change. And in the kitchen, serving boarders,
his widow-in-waiting has no time to face her life
without him. August, and the oarsmen of the Fraser
pull away from wharves, following the banks. The
salmon come in as they have always done, fattening
the pockets of the few, Ladner, Ewen, English.
Somewhere in the marsh an abandoned scow rots
in the mud and rushes. The same warm breeze blows
there, and dies. It dies here too, suddenly, like
the breath on his cracked lips. No one knows he's
gone until the boarders have been fed, no one knows
his lungs at last have emptied of their silt.

IV

How many homes can a ghost call his to haunt?
Perhaps a younger shadow poles a Carolina stream.
Here, the natives find the souls of their dead in
every salmon fighting to return, and do not
need to stare a phantom out of mud and mist.
But the pull of these tides is stronger than
the colour of our skin. I have dreamed the grass
growing up around his Portland grave like rushes
through his barge's mossy ribs, and I have
read the faded label on his smithied tomb of tin.
But he's not lying where the Fraser doesn't flow.
His bones feel the swimming magnet of this coast.
We come back to where our blood was racing full:
Deas is here because the cycle claims us all.

HELL'S GATE: 1913

That year, the dead outgaped the stars; they did not blink
with each soft dawn, but turned their cold faces full to the
rotting sun. Thirty million sockeye swimming home, the Fraser's
largest recorded return. Banks along the mouth festered with
flesh the canneries could not handle; scows sunk to the water-
line were roped to docks heaped knee-high with stiff bodies,
and still the skiffs arrived, fishermen rowing mountains of
silver against the current, day after day, as though they'd
opened a vein in the silty bottom of the river. So much slaughter
poured from the canneries and spewed back on the tides that the
seagulls gargoyling the deadheads and pilings of Canoe Pass and
Port Guichon maintained an eery silence, their gullets gorged
with entrails, while miles away, the ivory-ankled debutantes
of Kitsilano beaches waded daintily through the offal of their
fathers' wealth. No one could ignore the dead of that summer.
But a greater massacre lay ahead.

130 miles upstream, where the Fraser Canyon constricts to
its narrowest point, rock from illegal railway-blasting high
in the mountains choked the channel. By early August, with the
river low, a school of salmon stretched 26 miles downstream,
waiting to leap again into the chasm that thundered and sprayed
between the cliffs. But many were dead already, and the others
doomed. Packed together like seeds in a pomegranate, they could
not get across to spawn. The fruit of the season rotted fast,
washed back to Hope, filled every nostril with its putrid stench.
A few of the living tried to dig trenches for their eggs, but
the current was too strong, while the dead gave up their eyes
to the connoisseur hunger of the birds massed along both banks.
So many bodies they couldn't be bothered to turn them over
for the other eye. And the fish kept coming. New arrivals
plunged into the torrent, and fell back, again and again,
until they had no strength left. Springs, pinks, dogs, sockeye;
millions perished at the Gate. Major runs were wiped out, others

devastated to the point of extinction. Bloody footprints filled
the river and walked slowly back to the sea, pallbearing
the last rich August for generations.

At the mouth, the slaughter continued; cannery-crews worked day
and night to pack the catch; groups of men on wharves, in skiffs
and scows, raised their sharp gaffs against the sun, while
weary voices called out the growing numbers of the dead.

WEST COAST WINTER: 1942

He made the most beautiful duck decoys
in the province: handcarved and painted,
so lifelike they embarrassed the hunters
who tried to flush still coveys from the marsh.
Kenji and Deyo went out before the sun
in self-built punts of cherry wood
to gather the drifting canvas for their father's art:
Mr Okeda, barber to the round-eye and Chinee,
escaped from the Emperors in 1905,
escaped from the CPR mountain crews,
escaped from the river-steamer deckhand's life
of toting maggoty green hides along slippery wharves,
every evening put down his scissors for a knife,
left whorls of cedar like a blonde child's curls
in the long grass by the smokehouse,
held dead mallards on his knee to capture
all the bird's intricate colours and shapes,
sat for hours in flickering coal-oil light
perfecting the shift of a tail, the puffiness of cheeks,
the natural narrowing of the eyes,
sat in silence carving masterful lies
while the darkness around him filled
with soft, white shavings of smoke.

All that year, trainee-pilots in Tiger Moths
formed frightening flocks above the Pacific;
until one cold morning in early December
two planes clipped wings and crashed
and the parachutes sank in the current's heavy drag
like dandelion seeds, and disappeared.
Late Halloween ghosts in Mr Okeda's chair,
tricked out in bedsheets stolen from the wash,
trembled underneath his blade with haunted thoughts
of tragic death so close to Christmas;

he could feel the sensitivity burn in each scalp
but his own hands never shook.

The day the Mounties came to start
the deportation, they gave the orders
in Japanese: Kenji and Deyo gaped,
unable to follow, and fought back tears
as their father explained.
My father helped them store their decoys
in the skinning-shed, all their punts,
oolichan nets and muskrat traps,
and then they said goodbye.

It was April 1942 and my father was seventeen;
the HMCS *Discovery* berthed in English Bay
waited for his tread upon its metal decks,
and a few miles off, behind barbed wire
on the Pacific National Exhibition grounds,
ten thousand Japanese spies stood motionless,
tuned to the airwaves of a phantom Tokyo,
weeping their perfectly-painted tears
while violent flocks careered through the sky
and somewhere inexpert hands sheared crude wigs
off the skulls of the dead.

1958

A little blood left in the wheelbarrow
after my father pushed the last
of his salmon home from the wharf
mixes with the falling rain
this September evening:
the canneries aren't buying
so he buries his catch
load after load
in the garden for fertilizer;
the sky around his hands
is dark and sweet as the blackberries
dying in the fields nearby
as the blade of his shovel
sloshes deep in the earth
again and again and the rain
dilutes the blood in the wheelbarrow
a lighter red then pink
then almost clear
until there is no trace of blood at all
only the reflection of a young man's eyes
peering out like stars
beautifully indifferent to the dawn
and the lonely swimming of the long long years.

THE PHOTOGRAPH

for my mother

Uncherished in the family catalogue,
found creased, yellow-edged,
at the bottom of a shoe box
stuffed in a cupboard,
it speaks to me more than
all the others, and in a voice
I almost recognize, soft
and far away

Yet the scene itself is common
to those years:

In my sister's infant hand
a strawberry ice-cream cone blazes
like a torch, lighting up,
along the lily-pad float,
my father and teenaged brothers
shirtless in the April sun,
their bodies slim and pale
as three long cigarettes
as they pose, grinning,
beside a dead spring salmon,
sixty-plus pounds, held under the gills
by my father's strong, invisible grip:
beyond, the river is full of life
swimming towards a single purpose
high in the distant valley;
its calm is the calm
of chemicals in a darkroom sink,
poised for transformation,
the magic leap of images
drawn from nothing to the light.

It's taken me years to understand
why their happiness pains me:
youth cannot accommodate absence;
the woman's shadow on the mossy planks,
her thumb in the corner of the frame,
the date she'd written on the back
in a still-shaky hand
months after their loss:
it's taken me years to realize
the truest photographs never appear.

Soon, the pose dissolves,
the ice-cream melts down my sister's hand
in trickles, like the spring's blood
along its scales; the taut muscle
of my father's arm slackens,
his strong sons laugh,
and the tiny shadow within the shadow
turns naturally to the sound,
the salt of life already sweet
upon its mouth,
each perfect crystal another word
waiting to be voiced,
while the greater shadow,
river-still,
follows its own dark purpose
out of the frame.

Somewhere in a valley grave he's buried,
the one who took the bear's paw in his flesh
that I might surface to the sun,
who thrashed upon the tides of blood
that I might reach our common stream,
who turned too often in the net
and strangled on his joy;
yet still the one who whispers to me
of our human pain

when the salmon burst like flashbulbs
every spring along the coast
in a brilliant consecration
of the undeveloped souls who journey here.

AFTER PROUST

Nothing so delicate as a madelaine
but the smell of blood and oil takes me back
to those deep black waters and the salmon's silver
pause, deciding when to spawn and die,
a precious vein in solid coal
we mined with linen nets
lowered without beams
or the canary's saving song,
and my father still in the windless night
as a figure trapped in Pompeii's lava,
only the burning ash of his cigarette visible
sometimes falling from his face
like a molten tear or fiery mosquito,
his free hand light on the rigid corkline
as a butterfly settling onto pollen,
more sensitive than a nun's caress
on the brow of some feverish soul.
A hundred fathoms away, several fathoms
deep, the sockeye's instinct stirred
and kissed my father's hand:
"There's one, listen," his calm voice
followed by a short, soft splash
curiously detached from us
like the champagne bubbles of a suicide's dive
heard by revellers on the shore;
and swaddled on the deck in oily blankets
breathing the bloodied bilge, half-asleep
below the midnight's pale and distant stars,
I'd count until my eyes were closed,
"that's one, that's two, that's three"
and finally drift away.

No chestnut blossoms perfuming
shadow-dappled country roads,

no musk of leather reins and horses
whisking secret lovers into dawn,
no coffees and no cognacs
in small cafes along the route,
no lilac-scented boudoirs,
no letters and no lace,
no aristocracy, no king

except my father took
ten thousand kisses to his hands
from those he'd later kill
and wore their blood just like a Bourbon
in his long, dynastic gaze
as I counted all the heads that fell.

A glorious carnage takes me back
to the myriad molten tears
that fossilized the shadow
out of which I came,
to the daybreak's crimson sun
that rose above the mountains
like an angry cock to crow
the darkness from the deep

but even if I wrote a thousand volumes
and lived inside a cork-lined room
until my breath was stilled,
the numbers would stay lost:
the river's silver abacus resists
my touch, the Pompeii dogs refuse to bark,
my father's hand has risen
from the stamen of its youth.

I can't quite hear my child's voice
recount the years, the tides, the catch,
though I journey down the distant stars
awash in blood and oil

to those deep black waters
where everything is past
and even the simpler dreams denied me.

TAKING TEA TO MY FATHER

One flashlight-beam in all the darkness flowing
from river and sky, one long bone in the earth,
the path of one tear cried in some endless grief.
I splayed such vision as I had upon the night,
the owl's eye in my left hand seeking
not to kill, but a bath of familiar moonlight
for my nervous wings. Yet I was the bold creator
of my world, pointing the hidden into life,
the rain like dark claws in the branches
overhanging the dead-end road I walked
to reach the gravel dyke, the tomcat frozen
beneath the burned-out streetlamp, sparkling
pools of blood in his stricken stare, the torn
nets racked along the wharf like hammocks
for the fitful sleep of kelp-garbed ghosts;
even the river lived or died according
to the flight of my avian hand; I had a god's mind
in my wrist, and a child's fear.

But always, at the gangway descending,
where the tide flapped its loose black tongue
beneath the mossy planks, I saw the burning
coal-oil of the open netshed
blaze like a drive-in movie screen
on which the same dark figure, hunched,
intense and calm, smoked all being
into its shadow.

Then the owl's eye snapped shut: in my right hand
the thermos throbbed, blood-warm,
my small heart, love's prey, my own red life
fluttering down.

SECOND HOME

(setting out to fish the prairie drift at night)

Named for my sister, my parents' only daughter, the *Nola J*
idled so quietly up the vein-narrow sloughs of the lower Fraser
River, the porcelain poise of herons feeding in tidal pools
never once cracked into jigsaws of flight, and we could hear
the westerly wind with its backward glance forming pillars
of salt, grain by grain, in the marshes. Even the wake
was soft, a black butter spread between the banks;
it fell away from us, the same as August suns and summer
holidays, gently, like the lapping of an old dog's tongue
in a bowl of rainwater and blossoms. We might have been
drifting on a cargo of pollen-drunk bees bound for the comforts
of dusk and sweet combs, we might have been borne on the sigh
of a century, one hundred lost years in search of a current
to carry them home to the pages of history. Drowse, drowse,
and the wandering flotsam of all forgotten time; so we idled
with the idling of a young girl's name, and did not note
the frantic truth: no matter how many safe harbours you leave
as a child, the tide washes you back on the shoals of your age.

Nola, your boat is ash. We have a few pictures of the deck and
nothing else. But it's enough. Freshet of vision, freshet of
memory, we look back across the bows of every name those hours
whispered to us, and find small hives of sugar floating
through the marshes.

STRIKE

The stench of rotted herring can't be broken
with the fists of angry men, I know that much,
the current that drowned my childhood friend
cannot be turned by protest songs or shouts
our fathers hurled against the cannery walls,
whatever tears my mother wept when poverty
made her understand the thin soup-bones of
her mother's wrists—o buried in the eastern
snows—cannot be dried with 3 cents more per
sockeye pound wrung from stones of rich, red
blood; but those cursing men who walked our
midnight streets carrying vials of acid
like mad scientists to pour on the nets
of scabs believed their fists and songs
and hard-earned pennies were the means to
something better than endless drifts of
skunks and snags, and the chilblained hands
of winter works. We're all the living body
of someone's old belief. So if your father,
like my own, was proud enough to moor his
meaning for your dreams, and if your mother
also scrimped to keep your belly full, and
your childhood streets one night belonged
to human voices raised against a human wall,
then taste this air of rotted fish for what
it is, the life their worry saved you from,
the blood of all our private Spains
soaking up the moon.

OLD FISHERMEN: 1973

Their eyes have no colour in the coal-oil light
but still the moon knows them, as their long-dead
mothers would, by the hunch of a shoulder as they
bend to grab a hanging-needle from the wharf or
lean against the darkness when a dog downriver
howls to be fed. The moon has chalked their corpses
on these mossy planks and slowly hangs their final
days with its rope of muddy tides, but if they feel
the tightened noose, it must be made of all the silt
they've jewellered from the river-floor, so soft their
doom rests on them in this barge-slow summer night.

The current, dark as kerosene, and high, burns
with the flicked matchheads of the stars. It presses
fire into the soles of their gumboots, but they no
longer care to snuff the dangers of their world.
The snags and their blood have no separation; even
their shadows swim away from them like muskrats;
they know the air that blights the scarlet of the
salmon's flesh also eats a white path to their bones:
when they leave, they will kick the gravel of the dyke
until they're home, calmly dreaming of their ashes
floating out to sea, with the freshet, the fry, the
melted pawprints of the lynx.

I have no business to watch them mend their only
lives; their hands, heavy and scarred as tombstones,
gather the torn meshes soft as cream, wind the needles
through without pause, and pile perfect fathoms
for the dawn to find. They work with a touch
gentled by the final breath of frantic beauty.
I am younger than their nets, I can almost fit
through the holes the dying chinooks made,
but the distant water doesn't call my blood;
the canyon-walls have yet to narrow for my climb.

Now the pale knots of the moon begin to loosen
as the voices fade. Hangman, slip the hood of
summer softly on them, rope each face without
a burn, whisper, whisper sweetly as a mother,
let us feel the darkness loves them, let the
darkness smile at us through their nets of
silenced blood.

SOCKEYE SALMON

They move from the medieval to the Elizabethan
in a few short weeks. Pewter chalice, flashing
tip of the jousting lance, breastplate of kings:
silver and the subtle red, the surface that hints
at the vital hidden life, like the summer armour
of the maple leaf. Theirs is the brightness
of a dark age, lust plunging after grails,
appetite in clashing legions on a long crusade.
Try to stop them, and the gills fly up like shields,
spilling a blood so thick you can braid it into rope.
And the eyes never stop believing in the holy purpose
of the flesh; they know their dying is divine. Hold
the clotted rope, toll the battered monastery bells:
you can't kill their naked century with the hollow
ringing of a human time.

But let them pass. They will make the abdicating
leap themselves, from instruments of god to capering
fools. Green-capped, in scarlet hose, they leap into
their final hours, laughing with the rapids, always
pushing their comic luck against the claws of power.
With a hey-nony-nony the sharpest minds can't fathom.
No one understands their ancient irony. Out on the savage
heath, alone, exiled from the court, they only make it
back to feel the planet's executing spin; blood beneath
the scaffold for the leering crowd, empty eyes catching
a twinkle of starlight, their final riddle, finest joke.
Already their tears are growing into a brilliant future,
down beneath the gravel. They are singing the strength
back to earth, and the belief. The sun has murder on
its hands, and so do we. But the lakes are full of song.
The rivers open like a great hall, the ocean is a castle
we can't storm. History says "love the flesh, your gods,
die well." Or "laugh your way to a permanent glory."
Century by century, year by year, this is the sockeye's
gift of paradox. Take it. And let your living tell.

DOG SALMON

The feds call them chums, but they are no one's friends.
Their jaws are so strong, their teeth so sharp, it's as though
the forgotten muskrat traps of all our sloughs had suddenly
decided to spawn a brighter steel somewhere in the mountains.
In early fall, they move upriver like a rainbow made of flesh,
their large, olive bodies wrapped in bright purple bands;
we drift over them, no song on our lips, no dreams of potted
gold, just a silent determination not to rip our hands apart
when we pick them from the net. From late October on, the rainbow
fades to ugly storm; they grow black as the pilings of ruined
canneries, drive forward like pounded railroad spikes. No one
wants their meat by then; it goes to feed the hungry dogs from
whom they get their name. And even though they have no bark,
their bite takes weeks to heal. Rumour says they've broken wrists
with one quick jerk, and that they hang on logbooms with their
teeth to rest against the tide. Try to kill them at your peril.
Fact says they fight as hard as any human not to die.

JACK SPRING

I

Advance scouts.
Immature lookouts too small
to fight. But never turn away
from them. They offer a chance
at the big brass, the chinook,
the medal-heavy generals. If
you catch one in your net, go
slow. Do not pick it out at
first, just rest it gently in
the stern. Forget the pedal for
the drum: now you'll need your
hands and nerve. Lean across the
rollers, peering down. Pull the
meshes one by one, and sniff the
air for heavy musk, the scent
of fresh-snapped thyme. Often,
a giant shadow hanging by a tooth
will dare your gaff-hook aim.
Advance scouts. But never for the
journey, only for the death. It's
a rare force, earth's sole democracy,
commoners bleeding in the moonlight,
their bodies heaped with royalty.

II

We always take them home. Perfect
meals for the elderly widow up the street.
Flesh as red as their blood. Backs speckled
as night skies in winter. Bones fine and
hard enough to be toothpicks. We always
take them home. There we go now, walking
wearily down the Ladner dyke in summer

darkness, hooking a week of suppers for
a lonely woman in our fingers, swinging
them like railway lanterns at the scene
of a wreck, while behind us, in the hold,
the chinook smolder in their heavy smoke.

STEELHEAD, SPAWNING

What we dreamed of when young, but never found,
comes in with the tide tonight. What we loved,
but lacked the will to pursue, moves swiftly
in the mouth. Beautiful ghost, blushing
in the gills, the saltmarsh sighs to see
your rare body beacon the night. What have
we done to yesterday? The river flexes its
last wild muscle, strong and sure. Casts
its bright hook in our sleep, and pulls.
While we rise to the unbreathable element
of loss again.

DOLLY VARDEN

This should have been the name of my first girlfriend, not
first death, someone to practise my windmill pitches with
in the last long light of August suns, those little red wagons
pulled by dusk, someone whose silver laughter swam
the fields, whose leaping body twisted in its one true
element, blood like lava, the unglazed eye,
life in the heat of a dying summer, in the blackberried
air, the dripping musk.

There was no girl. The only bearer of that name
flashed its perfect silver on the muddy riverbank
a painful quivering moment before the rushes sighed
"that's done." I had never touched the blood of another
species, my hands were starlight still searching
the darkness for eyes to fill. Imagine! They hung
in the morning-rain like white roses, the sky
breathed lightly on them, it didn't know the day
had cut the stems.

What element is ours? I wish that name had been
a girl's, I wish she'd thrown a thousand pitches back
to me before my touch could rouge the ball. Pretty
to dream, summer's tiny wagons loaded down
with fresh-cut grass, pretty to dream, laughter
in forgotten fields, first love, and the gift
of the only roses a woman should desire, handed
shining out of the darkness where our blood is made.

STURGEON

I

We believe them ancient, prehistoric,
their strangely-whiskered, small-eyed faces
like those of Oriental villains
in silent movies, floating up
from currents of opium to sell
sweet girls into slavery;
we believe them alien, mysterious,
royals of a remote dynasty
reigning over the muddied depths,
at bliss in a bubbling dream.

We believe because
we seek some distance
from their power, the gaze
that mocks our blood's short course:
seventy years! the bones
poke through our skin like sandbars
at the lowering tide;
we can't love long enough
to penetrate their thick, drugged world,
that haze of silt
falling in the riverbottom's eery light
like dust in a streetlamp's glow:
we fear their exotic ugliness
for in it shines
the commonplace beauty of loss.

II

One autumn night in the early seventies
at the mouth of the Fraser River
800 pounds of history woke
from its long, blind sleep

to wear my father's finest meshes
across its eyes
like a bridal veil
and jilted a dozen other men
before it slept at last
the century in a nylon coffin
gasping at the nearness of the stars:
roped to the stern, dragged against
the tide till drowned,
the years left a dark swath
in the dark waters:
"Winched on the wharf," my father said
quiet over his morning coffee
as I delayed my walk to school,
"it looked like a beam of moonlight."

III

Most often now, they're young,
three pounds or four,
just past being a delicacy
on the tongues of the rich:
imagine a child's living eyes
in the face of a dead man,
imagine history condensed to seconds
hung like lizards in the drifting air:
pulled from the net, in our hands
they twist for freedom; are we
an exotic ugliness they have come
to fear? Can our gaze reflect
a loss beyond our own?
Released, their tiny bellies
flash pale in the green tide,
shards of an old moonlight
destined never to stir
the silts of the kingdom.

IV

My father at seventy
still remembers
the great sturgeon
tall in the chill air
as a tower of bone:
"I couldn't believe,"
he often says
"how something so white
could cast such a dark shadow."

And we stare into the river
one man
waiting for the black
to lift from the earth,
brushing, with a single thought,
the soot from our trailing selves.

OOLICHAN

Everything is dark in the town along the rivermouth.
One light only moves over the dyke, past the fishboxes
and crab-pots piled ten-high, a zoo of cages trapping
the black hiss of the current and nothing more, into
potholed streets still untouched with the wild cherry's
first glimmer of blossom. One dull-silver light pulled
from the last good tide and poured into a bucket
where it still trembles, just slightly. One light
between the harbour and Port Guichon, between the
mossbacked netsheds and the bat-filled barns, one
light for the rushes, the same for the fields,
so carefully carried you can almost hear
the gills of summer closing on the cold salt
fathoms so far from home. And in the light, one hand,
strong, veined like the delta, forming a fist
over the bucket-handle. A hand off a da Vinci oil.
The light on the hand, the hand in the light;
in this almost total darkness the tiny masterpiece
of an unsung Renaissance swings gently, rises and
falls and moves slowly across the lower sky.

I will not begin to claim I know the source
of any light or understand the strength that
brings it to us in our dreams. It is enough
to find a quiet beauty on my doorstep when
I wake, to feel the wire of the handle in
my palm like a cold vein, to brave the weight
of brilliance ancient as the glacier-pools.
It is enough to take from hand to hand
the quiet energy the river conducts
and pass it down, like silt, through
the warm, red estuary of every living touch.

BULLHEAD

Cruelty named him for his resemblance
to an ugly groundfish; he had the same
bulging eyes, thick lips, and roughskinned face,
and seemed more than willing to feed
his voracious appetite for acceptance
down at the murky bottom of the world.
The unangelic crowd he curried favour with,
heavy drinkers at fifteen, their cigarette-smoke
haloes made blacker by the "fuck this,
fuck that" poetry of pool hall and netshed,
roped him to pilings and, laughing, disappeared
until the muddy tide had lapped his quickened breath,
or lassoed him around the neck, hitched the free
end to the bumper of a truck, and drove
just fast enough to make him run and fall and
shred his knees for miles on the gravel roads
outside of town, or simply bloodied his face
so often, his nose became a tap turned on
at will by a well-placed fist or knee.

Five years behind at school,
I mostly heard about these things, and perhaps
that was the joy for him, the minor fame
he won in place of love; I couldn't say.

Though once I stood beside him on the wharf,
and with a dozen other kids watched him chew
a salmon's eyes, and swallow, until I had to look
away before I retched: he did it on a dare
for two-bits and a chocolate bar.

Now I read he's dead at thirty-five,
or at least his christian self,
"suddenly," which I take to mean

(for old times' sake)
a haemorrhage or overdose.

It doesn't really matter:
Bullhead with the red, raw scarf
around his throat
has run into the ground at last
with a muddy kiss upon his rotten lips
and the blinking stars and mocking laughter
won't come back
though all his swallowed eyes are swimming mad
inside the earth, still lanterning the darkness
for our childish love and adult tears,
whatever the hell our tears are worth.

THE LAST SOCKEYE

for my brother

Always I think of the last sockeye,
the one in late October: blind,
blood-red, half-rotted, so far
from the creeks of spawning,
it just lay beside our net
in the silt-grey water—confused
or resting, we couldn't say—
then with one weak push
gilled itself
so we had to roll it in.

The last of its kind for the season;
most had died, or spawned and died,
at least a month before:
though barely caught, I could not gaff it;
we stood in the chill north wind, bemused,
as though we'd been given an early Christmas gift,
red-wrapped and taken
from below the mountains' undecorated evergreens;
we stared at the rotted eyes
and scales like bloodied coin,
a glove of chain-mail
after a Crusades slaughter
the living hand still inside.

Three separate instincts
and a whole long winter to forget
your drinking and failed marriage
my loneliness and too often
days of great despair
over things I cannot change

and always the gap between us
as wide as the gap
between the sockeye and its goal;
three separate instincts
with nothing to win
three separate species:
I don't remember what we said
or even if we spoke at all
but the salmon, at least,
knew what it wanted,
so I gave it back to the river,
blind, rotted, and doomed,
I gave it back

while we stood in the stern like the last men
and watched the bloody hand of the year wave goodbye

POKER

The best hand my father ever played
he slapped down slowly on the deck
of a Canadian Fish Company collector
one brisk fall morning in the mid-sixties:
four red springs caught in the night,
each exactly 52 pounds, silver and black,
four "big pigs" that stunned the other
players standing on the *Maureen G*
into cries of disbelief as the two boats
spun in a back-eddy just above the wharf
at Wilkies Island. From what dark sleeve
of coincident doom he pulled those rare,
red aces, no one knew; they only stared
with mounting awe as one by one he raised
each heavy body from his hold and then
returned for more. But even he could not
accept the perfect balance of his cards,
that they should be exactly matched.
Four times the scales showed 52, and when
the last spring weighed the same, no one
spoke for fear the river hid a secret hand
below its flowing surface, and would show it
in another game less kind to human wiles.

We have nothing up our sleeves; the largest spring
we've caught in years has barely tipped the scales
at thirty pounds, and even that was white. I'm sure
the fear that bound the mouths of older men in
other seasons was the fear their breath might marry
to the deepest silt: we perceive a slower doom.
My father and the packer-crew read no future in
the bloody tarot spread upon the deck; they picked
the smaller dead into the scale, and then went home
to sleep. We deal in barren years. History calls,
the future folds. There's little left to read,
a paradise to weep.

MIDNIGHT

A seal shrugs her soft shoulders in the wind
a few fathoms from our boat
as if to say she understands;
her eyes are the colour of hot chocolate
thick with milk; starlight flecks them
like an exotic spice
stirred in by the tides off Asia;
her whiskers are wet with moonlight
like a cat's in a cream-bowl,
her skin is a brindled shammy
in the hands of a lonely child
kept after school for daydreaming;
she is still in the dark river
as a tombstone no one visits,
she is a hitchhiker's thumb
held out in the air
of a deserted highway,
she is the shadow
of a small planet we've overlooked
just beyond the sun

and when she cries at last,
full-throated, head raised,
the blood of her pup
flows warm again through my hands
as though I'd been sifting the salt
from a lifetime of human tears
and did not know I had cried them.

YOUNG EAGLE ON A PILING

We had thought to drift so far
meant no witness but the wild sea
and the last glazed gape
of dying salmon slicked
in their own blood at our feet;
we had thought to feel our bones
pull anchor from our flesh
as shore and safety fell away
meant an isolation known
perhaps to saint and sacrifice
but not to common men:
black clouds scraped across the sky
behind which a few stars in
their pale youth stared down
pitiless. Yet we could not accept
the casual coming of the night,
how it deepened so slowly
like the blush on a grape,
how it swept over the waters
in a silent tide, dragging
its corkline of distant worlds,
its giant ghostly buoy;
we could not believe in death
of such a soft arrival

Until at the river's final marker,
a decayed piling looming just beyond
our bow, like a scorched stake
kindled by the flesh of suns,
we felt the hour's essential hunger
pierce our skin, we felt
for the first time
our slicked hearts thrashing
in our hands: there,

calmly perched against the wind,
his feathers ruffled like the water's surface,
a young eagle looked beyond ourselves
to the darker simpler facts
of fear, and what they meant
to his survival. For only a second
out of the gloom, we met
his steady yellow gaze, beacon
to a shore we had no wish
to touch, and then, as quick,
the night consumed the piling
and its patient guest

Later, the net picked up at last,
the still catch gasping in the stern,
we trained a spotlight on his perch
but he had gone,
dark ash of the day's staked sun
scattered in the storm,
raised anchor of the seeking blood
dragged across the stars,
black soul, pure need,
the truth our pretty lives
had drifted from

CANOE PASS

Driftwood wakes me, thumping the hull
like called spirits. It is the brief,
closet-close darkness of early summer,
and six mast-lights gild the towhead.
I step out of the cabin to breathe
and check the tide. Still running out,
a wet rope dropped to the bottom of a
well. The six boats tear at their anchor-
chains like rabid dogs. Deadheads, logs,
branches, black shapes against the black,
flash into the dim sheen, then disappear,
rushed to the sea. No one sets at the
Brunswick now; a radio left on squawks
once, its echo dying in the marsh. On
the far bank, a single light burns in
a farmhouse, someone reading late or
worrying. I have been that profile,
the slow pace on hardwood floors;
my heart has beat against the windowpane
like a bird drawn to its own image.
We are never on the earth.

The wind rises and falls, last breaths
in the side of a wounded deer. I am
one step from the black graves flowing
by, one beat from the broken glass.
It's July, past midnight, in a narrow
channel where the salmon run. I know
how easily I could lose the stars,
vanish quietly as a page turned by
sleeplessness. Who watches, save
the dead, our second at the rope?

But it is gone, as fast. The wind shifts,
a scent of fresh-cut pea-vine wafts in
off the fields, and a distant figure crosses
the sky to sleep. All along the coast, dark
wings are folding, clear of glass. Praise
the running out, and the low water slack,
our life is a thunder that chooses its clap.

APRONS

Different maps of the same country dried
on my parents while they worked. In the kitchen
my mother swept damp hair from her forehead
as she checked the gauge on the pressure-cooker
and wiped the bright red continents of our
winter survival on her aproned waist. Then
back to the sink to peel more tomatoes, gut
more sockeye, smear new borders to our world.
Even the moon, so small outside, only dared
a peek through the corner of the window, for
fear the knife would slice her light.
At the same time, on the river, my father
drifted wildly towards the sea, a faint glow
catching the last mad strokes of each gasping
cartographer he wrenched from his net. Sweating,
cursing the speed of the tide, his own fingers
never swift enough, he had no control over the
borders nature drew upon his life, our lives.
Then back upriver for another set, his aproned
chest rich with violent lands. And the moon,
unafraid, swelled in his bloodshot eyes.

I can see my parents still, leaning above
their worlds, the steam dampening my mother's
hair, the wind whipping spray into my father's
face, their two aprons quietly charting
the country I was born to leave, and the moon
like the naked ghost of the earth, whispering
strange tomorrows at my shoulder.

SKULLCAPS

The dogs were in the river when the Greek boy drowned
along with his crew-mates in the northern waters.
We knew him, knew his family. His death made the
frost deeper; the gangway leading from the low tide,
the gravel dyke, the road back to our house; everywhere
a young face drained of colour. I was six, moored
to my father's pantleg, lost in a forest of dark
shapes cast by other men. Their five o'clock shadows,
cigarette smoke, and sober talk of seiners going down
in distant straits made me shiver more than the chill
October day. I remember they all wore skullcaps, my
father too, and suddenly removed them in one shared
motion. The dead boy's aunt, dressed head-to-toe in
black, carried her still veil slowly through the awful
whiteness of the world. She passed below us, on the road,
like a mutant wave torn from the choppy currents where
her nephew clutched his final star. I peered around my
father's duffel coat and saw the deep hole torn in the
middle of his chest. The others had it too. Their lowered
skullcaps made a black bouquet for death's grim courting.
The woman went by, silent and dark as the salmon
pushing their blood through the sloughs. The men didn't
speak again until she'd disappeared, just drew deeply
on their cigarettes and coughed. Then they lifted all
the absence gathered in their hands, and put it on.
Clutched pieces of the only night they feared.
I remember it was October, very cold. We took
our shared blood home, and my father steered.

GUMBOOTS

The first dug foot of every grave
gapes each night on the thirty porches
of my past. I am far away from
that last journey, gods be kind,
but I know the men who step deeper
into death and walk their endings
to the wharf. And when they pull
the soil to their knees, I know
the strength that lets them drag
it to the river. And I also know
the hands of women on their shoulders
like patches of warm sunlight holding
them up. The tiny marionetting bones
that keep their flesh alive. Thirty
men knee-deep in the earth
walk heavily to the end of summer.
Thirty sleepless nights go with them.
While the porchlights beat a soft morse
to my roaming fathom.

GAFF-HOOKS

The sheaves are not golden where we reap.
The field is not still. We slice our hands
through a silver motion; there's blood in
the grain that falls at our feet. And death
is too busy dying to be a perfect symbol.
Each season asks "why extend your touch
if not to love?," and each season passes
without an answer. I have been reaching
with a sharpened hand all my life. I will
reach again this summer, and the next.
The salmon will hang beneath the rollers,
poised for a final lunge. The dark blade
of the current will sweep below us all.
"Why extend your touch if not to love?"
To be grain in the August sun, perhaps,
to be a field for the light, to fall.

TIDEBOOK / FISHBOOK

My family's only first editions,
slime-stained, wind-cracked,
opened and read in all weathers,
tossed down on the boot-printed floor
of our moving library. Each year,
new copies, and the same story told
with only slight variations; low water
on the fourth of August that much lower,
37 sockeye delivered instead of 46:
but we were co-authors with the river
of that second book and filled its pages
with the nerve-ends of our hours.
Under shelves of stars,
my father wrote his living down, under
the bulb of summer suns, his muscles
made the numbers and the words that kept us
fed. But he created only what the first book
gave, the salt sea pushing at his hold, the
river pulling to the sea. We knew the tides
could make a pauper out of any floating king.

Those soaked and sunburned volumes ended
every season in a box of snarled mesh and
union tags. Thirty years of flow and catch
my father buried in his shed. Thirty years
of looking through the words to better read
the life he chose to live. And now my hands,
like his, are pages smeared with scales and
slowly turned, high water, low water, backup
and runoff, the heavy, bone-spined history
that every human eye is born to read and never
understand. Gaze at the bleeding ink beneath
your skin, and ask, where is the river that
grants me mercy, where is the book my heart
has bound with sinews of the tide and wind?

SMOKEHOUSE

My first real kiss tasted of burnt chinook
and cherrywood. I won it in a smokehouse
on the banks of the Fraser River, circa 1975.
When I stepped out of that narrow darkness,
the scent of summer's spent desire on my skin,
October threw my shadow farther than I'd ever
thrown a stone; I could not see the far bank
of my own body, I could not hear my senses
splash on the other side. Along the fence,
the tall corn whispered secrets, and a cat's
eyes swallowed a robin whose heart thrummed
thunder from a distant rooftop. Was another
shadow running an arm to soreness in the grass?
I did not look. My eyes had dropped like stones
into the river, and the current pulled them deep.
Somewhere up the valley, wind flayed the flesh
of salmon hung in the rocks, dried it to ribbons
pink enough for a schoolgirl's hair. Tongues
would tease it for flavour in another season,
and go silent in the tasting. But that day,
the clouds poured east in a rich smoke, faster
and faster, hunger of the earth for heaven,
hunger of the air for blood, hunger of the blood
for burning. Now, I stay my arm to listen.
These words step out of a high dark,
and there's fury in their swimming.

AFTER LEARNING MY GIRLFRIEND MIGHT BE PREGNANT

My bones are trapped moonlight that fell a thousand years before anything drew breath on this planet. They float in my skin, wanting release, wanting to bend the tall marsh grass with the weight of their longing. I have carried them here, to my favourite small island in the rivermouth, gingerly, as though I were trying to move a dewdropped web without waking the spider, as though my heart might open any second, like a bloodshot eye, to watch the pale foundation of my life escape.

It's a warm morning in late May. I walk the narrow, winding trails shadowed by giant silver birches and cloudhigh poplars whose branches spill the weary sighs of last century's fishermen onto a soft breeze wafting in from the Gulf. Ahead of me, moving in and out of the spattered sunlight, a middle-aged woman, two small boys, and a cocker spaniel form an ever-widening circle of noise and colour, a pinwheel that eventually revolves out of sight as I take a different trail.

Soon I step out of the semi-darkness and arrive on the sparsely-treed edge of the island where all is mud, sand, bullrush and beached stumps. The tide is low, the river like ash dusted with a fine blue pollen of sky. Rings of charred driftwood mark the teenagers' weekend parties and a few beer bottles flash intermittently, lighthouses directing the mud-wasps back to their nests. It is too early for salmon. Their frenzied blood still masses out at sea, waiting to burst under the summer's full moons. Far away, in the mountains, bald eagles stare sleepily into clear creeks, only bothering to open one eye.

When I cross the sandy clearing between the river and woods, my bones begin to shimmer. They press their light into my throat, gathering it beneath my tongue. Suddenly, a small bird darts out of the marsh grass (combed over the sand like long hairs on a balding scalp) and half-flies, half-runs across my path.

It is a female killdeer. She approaches to within three feet, feigning a broken wing, and tries to lead me in another direction. Her efforts are frantic but keep to the same simple pattern. A series of high-pitched cries, a crazed dance towards me, then an awkward escape on a collapsed wing. I stop, knowing how close I must be to her nest. Out of the corner of my eye, the pinwheel spins, and I realize with some sadness that the jaws of the spaniel won't be locked with moonlight.

I am thirty years old. In two months I'll be wearing the soft red gloves the salmon weave when dying. I don't know if my bones will have returned to the earth they dream of touching, I don't know if they will have poured from my mouth with the words of a boy or of a man. I can see the black river like a sack full of blood, I can hear the fresh sighs dripping on the air; my body is bent to the task of killing, and the full moon weighs on my back like a hump. Is one shoulder lower than the other? Do I cry? Do my bones dance frantic in the cold approach of stars?

Looking Home, Sad as the Rain

I have gone further than the salmon now,
out of the Fraser Canyon, leaving Hope
behind, with its ring of sheer mountains
like a torn, blue dawn that never breaks
to full light, and the teenaged girl
shivering outside the Greyhound station
blown like a leaf of frayed denim through
the empty streets, her eyes big and wet
as fishbowls, and the minnow in each
darting wildly against the glass until
it seemed her thin body must shatter.
Now beneath those slick walls
the tender hearts of the sea hurry home
to die, and the jaws that will shred them
drift down from the peaks like a hard snow.
But these aren't my children; they're only
the years I have lived, massing again
in their dark shallows.

I have gone further than the death
I was born to know, away from the trembling
river inside each river. But the veins
in my wrists are the same colour as the
mountains rising above Hope, the same
colour as the veins in the wrists of
the two men searching for old fishnet
in the sharp rocks along the Fraser
who found instead the gagged body
of a young woman missing for weeks.
There is no world so vast as hunger.
Here, the streets are full of naked jaws
and the sky keeps sending them down. My
own is hard and moving. I have not gone
so far I can't taste the salt in the open

wound of my smile. The blue dawn in my body
shivers near breaking but will not usher in
a gentler light. Something tender has
come home to die and always will. This
is the distance the salmon journey.
This is the distance our dying knows.

Edmonton

TIDES (A POEM TO MYSELF)

Steal a rowboat tonight. Unlasso the mooring
that holds you to the shore. It's spring and
twilight and all the flowering cherries of
the earth have come on like pink streetlamps
to shed softness on your rainsweet ways
to the riverbank,
but do not linger as you might have
once, dreaming of french girls in their boudoirs
powdering a desired cheek; leave that
for the hockeymad boys levelling the grass
of vacant lots with scarred Sherwoods,
let them practise the loneliness
they need to perfect;
yours is already a statue marbled
by the moon, and stands in a field
where owls drag the darkness for suicides,
where the grave of each small shadow
they leave in the night
fills slowly with bones.

Instead, take the oars gently
as you would the arms of someone you love:
they're weightless, but the journeys inside
whisper with a heft only the intimate touch
understands. Now plunge your own still map
into the drifting ashes, and row.
If the oarlocks creak, imagine doors opening,
if your rhythm is off, keep time
to the motes of dust that tap your skin.
Soon, a muskrat will splash down
from the marsh, one black key played
on the piano, and a heron will briefly hang
its soft blue linen from the first faint star:
when this happens, do not be distracted;

arrive at the place where the current
runs strongest. And rest.

Breathe deep. Let darkness sink the world.
Let the stevedoring wind
load a freight of scentless blossoms
in the stern. The tides will bear it to the sea
and, somehow, bring you back alone,
with the blood your heart has yet to make
compass and anchor
for every mortal voyage
your unheld arms have just begun to dream.

FOR AN UNIDENTIFIED BODY FOUND FLOATING IN THE FRASER RIVER

I'm sorry
your fifteen minutes came too late,
that the paparazzi on the riverbank
flashed photos of your final pose
and did not beg for more,
that only the cattails sighed with longing
huddled together in the bitter wind
like Valentino's mourners,
I'm sorry
your police escort passed silent through the streets
and no one sought your autograph,
that coroners will touch you with a tenderness
perhaps you never knew in life, wondering
at a childhood scar or broken bone
that didn't heal exactly right,
I'm sorry
if attention's what you needed
such homage wasn't there.

But tomorrow, next week, whenever
the world has learned your sex,
your age, and all the folders close,
when the currents run without your weight
upon them like an added touch of moon,
when no one still remembers
the sudden taste of salt
your floating shadow brought
to sweetened air,
I will know the dark between
the logbooms where they found you,
and the long, slow sinking
of your nameless voice to silt.

RIVERMOUTH

Nets drift into herds here, corks and web
bunch around the hooves of Holstein cattle
as they graze, and bell-buoys clang
with every lowing. Ask a local farmer
who strides along the dyke; he'll say
the salmon are a moving crop, the tides
a rushing row. Dream too long on a tractor,
or fall asleep on a slack, and the dust
you breathe will fill with moisture,
cornstalks twine around your mast.
Here, we walk the deck in gumboots caked
with earth, carry salmon home in burlap
sacks that held our winter feed of spuds,
return to the same stretch of river as though
it were a field we'd fenced with rushes, barbs
of starlight. Or else we trade our baling hooks
for gaffs to pitch a swimming yield. To live here
means desire, potatoes lusting for the sun,
sockeye mad for autumn death, and faces
peering fathom deep and acre far. Our heaven
and our hell lie twinned below.

Land of the long journey, the great return,
seed into stalk, seed into schools,
but we can never leave: home is the delta
we bear in each wrist, and red is the skin
of our shadows.

Westham Island

The shot pheasant in the frozen furrows
of the potato field burns the daybreak's only
campfire beneath the silent laughing of a
golden retriever; all along the riverbank, red-
winged blackbirds settle their ash and flame
on the pale tips of bullrushes bent scimitar-
shaped by the breeze; in the dark, salt-seeking
current, dog salmon thick as a man's thigh
thrust themselves against the flow.

The muscles of the hunter are already
home. His breath is the colour of the small
moon just going down beyond the whale-grey
barns and capillary branches of the poplar
trees. With his whole body, he understands,
home is to breathe the very light
you'll do your dying by.

Now the final embers fleck the lowered muzzle
of the dog; the hunter swings his smoking shotgun
like the censer of a Catholic priest
above the coffins of his dead:
the lights in a few farmhouses
come on, slowly, hearts flushed
with a love of common things.

ON THE DISAPPEARANCE OF TWO MILLION SOCKEYE SALMON

Tonight
the river is black as the pupil of a Spanish murderer.
Guilty men skulk along the dyke carrying burlap sacks
of mewling kittens while their children sleep. Gill-
netters named for long-dead women rub moss from broken
wharves while the poplars stand like quill-pens
saturated with a wordless ink.
A full moon floats above but can't be seen.
It has taken its light home. It has swallowed
its own tears, like an oft-beaten child
who finally gives up on love.

Tonight
the river is black as the pupil of a Spanish murderer
drifting through a moonless town with a knife in his grin.
The tossed sacks throb like hearts as they sink.
The ghosts of all women weep for their names
though so many lives will never be written
in the distant valleys of our longing.

Now a blue heron settles on the grass-tombed weighs
of an abandoned boatworks
and carefully counts each breath
that leaves its frail body.
There aren't enough.
There can never be
enough.

Far from here, the dawn,
like a rusty freighter,
drags its heavy chains across the sea.

A POSTCARD FROM BRITISH COLUMBIA TO NEWFOUNDLAND

It won't be long
before the salmon deny their flesh to ceremony
and our charred smokehouses sink like coffins
beneath the weight of stars no one navigates
their heartbeats by: already
the rivers of our province tremble
with the fevered gaze of grizzlies and
the bloodless casting of the eagle's claw;
already the slow snakes of blackberry bramble
crawl towards our drying-racks and lick
the salted mud of history from our hulls.
It won't be long
before the wakes we spread upon the sea
are merely tired caresses of a corpse
and the nets we mend in songless harbours
the unheard strumming of tuneless harps:
somewhere soon
the silver notes our fingers once possessed
will eke their spirits out in poisoned graves
so far from us
they might as well be dying on a different coast
where the only blood that spawns is human
and the mystery is never how
we swim our way to death, but why
our swimming hastens it.

Come, while the moon is gilled
and breathing in the darkness,
we will slip into our oilskins
one last time and descend
like burning candles to the shore;
it won't be long
before the vanished schools return
to feed upon our melting dreams.
Come, and if we're doomed
by the justice of the coldest stars,
we alone must be the constellation
of our final hours.

DESIRE

I

Even in summer
we know the salmon is its own hoary grave, staring
hard at eternity through the tiny black wreaths
of its singular vision. Warm August nights,
we gather the rising frost of the sea and toss
the sad tokens of its blind faith into piles
to be traded for garlands dulled by promiscuous
touch. Yet still we drift downriver, swallowing
full jars of blackberry darkness with each breath
while our slowed hearts sigh
"how near the exotic is to the known."

Only hours and ocean hide the Japanese sun
as it slips from the horizon like a silk kimono,
exposing the pure white stars, those million
shivers on a loved one's body.
If we were driftwood, we might reach them,
if we were the fallen crosses of the forest,
we might be lazied into tasting all the promised
mysteries of the moonspiced tides.

II

But there is a passion in us turned by the frost,
by the spreading rays of the winter sun called back
to the mountains: even as the swollen blackberries
drip like sizzling oil on the banks
we see the grizzly's stand in the chill rapids,
his thick shape nailed to the snowy peaks
by bloodhammered silver; we see him,
a fur-swaddled landlord of Imperial Russia
raising a half-eaten sockeye like a goblet of wine,
and if we stare long enough

we see the moment when he must turn to fish
in the still creek of his shadow,
when he must paw survival out of his bones.

III

Here,
to want the naked stars,
we must look through, and through again,
the blackness that our living spreads upon the earth;
we must kneel in the rime of the sea
and read the scarlet epitaphs each torn gill
limns on our hands;
we must accept our bodies are their own deep graves
and our blood tossed roses that the future tends
with summer, moonlight, tides,
but no more pity
than the salmon ponders through its wreaths.

SUNSET: LADNER HARBOUR

The end of the day, the summer, the season's
big sockeye run. One gillnetter, out for crabs,
idles in from the Gulf with a stern-load of full
pots. In the slow-flowing lava of the sun
I can see the crabs twitching like severed hands
as the boat moves past me on the dyke. I know
the man behind the wheel. Yet it seems impossible
to wave. Who would I be waving at, the man I am
or the hundred prisoned selves I can't become?
Suddenly it is so still along the channel
I can hear the ticking of a muskrat's heart
as he swims his worry home. The fisherman has
shut his engine off, and drifts into the wharf.
It is not a muskrat's heart. It is not even my own.
The crabs are waving like children on a schoolbus
bound for the rest of their lives. Everything is
ending in the world, going down, but I have chosen
to start from here, again. The broken hands click
their knitting-needles under the guillotined sun
and the seconds die quickly in the wristbones hanging
at my sides, but I have chosen a different course:
let the clutching of the dead bring down the sky;
I won't count the shreds of light they hold.
Something rises in us, despite the world.
This is not silence. The stars open their eyes
like waking children, and from the very bottom
of the sea, the gnarled hands of grandparents
introduce the hour with a soft applause.

FALL FISHING

At first we could see the evening sun, red
as the last sockeye spawning in a mountain
creek, and even when the mists rose from
the marshes and sloughs, surrounding
the light until it seemed the whole sky
had clouded over with milt, we did not
panic, but simply imagined a greater cycle
than the one our nets destroy year after year,
that the sun should die this way each night,
dramatically, and the mists be shaped into a moon
that would swim beyond the world, returning at dawn
with blood on its back to fire our dark horizon once again.

And then we lost both banks. Suddenly, our voices
had no bodies. As the drum turned, we looked down
at the corks slipping through our hands, but could
not see them. Soon, darkness deepened the obscurity;
we became each other's shadow, unveined and floating,
ash cooling in the mist.

October fog comes straight from the grave.
It is the breath of all who died love-less
and hating. Now we feel it on our necks,
in the corners of our eyes. Dew-glazed,
our bones shake like pilings on a fast tide,
threaten to break off and join the river's
furious descent to the sea. And somewhere
in the narrow throat of our drifting,
the season's fiercer salmon, jag-toothed
and clever, tear at our net the way dogs
yank bones from a pack. They refuse to dance
their deaths for our accounting, but hang by
a single mesh, and thrash, and make us rip
them from their lives. So no sound tells us

our direction. We strain to hear the current
claw a chunk of mud from the bank behind us,
or suck its rage around the decayed pilings
fixed like eyeless beacons to the farther shore,
but not even a coho's final gasp in our corkline's
vanished curves saws the soaking marble of our tomb.
We hover like spirits between the worlds,
devoid of purpose: in vain, our numb hands
brush the cobwebs from the swallowed stars.
Then a small voice whispers "pick up"
and the drum begins to turn again.

Now the dim glow of a single hanging bulb
picks us out of absence. Gowned by fog,
masked by breath, we lean across the metal rollers,
gaffing shadows more powerful than memory, piercing
the point of longing in the season's
mad-eyed dream to live beyond the roaming
seal-pack and the salt-rimed sloughs.
Minutes pass;
our wrists throb with the weight of each failure,
our fingers wear the slick stigmata of angered gill
and twisted jaw as we wrestle the dying
from the net and heave them underneath the drum
where they still move forward, jagged pieces
of the current.

We have forgotten the sky long since,
and the bloodbacked swimmer whose soft gills
flush pink above a distant, warmer earth;
we are figures in a nightmare that spins
without pause towards the blindest fathoms
of the open sea: behind us,
the slow, irregular heartbeat
of the salmon's fractured cycle bumps dully
on our wooden deck, and echoes, until we can't be certain
the awkward rhythm isn't ours, the black pulse also in

our flesh, counting out a longer doom, but just as sure,
as we drag our battered scotchman like a small dead sun
out of the murk, then idle up the hidden drift,
longing always for the born horizon,
the saltless, clearblue graves of coming home.

GUTTING

I scatter the news of atrocity
and slaughter across the cracked
linoleum of the kitchen floor:
on my knees, I carve off the coho's head
beneath the gills, then slit its pale
white belly like an envelope thick
with all the morning's reported blood;
my smeared hands know the long routine,
where the useless organs go, and if female,
how to freeze her pretty eggs for sale
to those who kill her swimming kind
another, slower way. It's the first
of November six short years from the
end of the millenium, and silent
but for the scraping of scales and
the small black breath of rain against
the window.

No one is home in the world.

Yesterday, on this same floor
with these same hands, I hollowed out
a pumpkin for the Festival of All Souls;
its insides were wet, stringy, and
the seeds as multiple as eggs;
orange clots splattered the bloated
bellies of starving children as I carried
my candled leer outside, a warm greeting
for all our precious ghosts.

But tonight has no design. Can you hear
the measured breathing of the earth?
I'm on my knees, the blade slices,
the coho gapes and gapes in the bottom
of a brown paper bag; I'll bury its rich,
red loss in the garden later, deep, under
the wet newsprint of the scattered moon,
and with my calm millenial gaze
gut the living future from the stars.

WINTER

Shhh. The season has ended. The green
blood has gone out of the rushes; they're
ruffled and pale as the necks of dead
herons, a million sad markers
for the grave of forever.
Shhh. The *Native Dawn* and the *Evening Star*
are moored and sleeping in the harbour;
their dark nets have slipped away like
the shadows of whales, their sonar tracks
starlight blown off course by the wind,
their bows murmur "Bella Coola"
and their sterns sigh "Home," weeping
scales and years.
Please. Be still. Tonight our hearts are rising
heavy with salt to peer through the open porthole
of the moon. Don't startle them
before that calmer sea is glimpsed.
Let your voice weigh anchor.
Please.
What can it possibly matter to you?
Love is a rough crossing.
We're all growing older.